<u>In & Out The BoxX</u>

A Collection of Unparallel Poetry

Bryce Jones

.:OPEN M!ND PR0DUCT!ONS:.

Copyright by Bryce Jones

ISBN 978-0-6152-0352-2

www.myspace.com/syzzy

(For really GOOD music)

Acknowledgments

Thank you to my incomparable, irreplaceable family, living & deceased,

And everyone I surround myself with outside of it.

Yall know who yall are. I love yall.

Without all of you there's no me.

And lastly I'll thank the universe by the way I live.

One Liz

THE LINE-UP

Powell Kline {Pt. 1}

Faith

Troubled

No Love

Dear You Know Who You Are

The Courtyard

Sorry D

Tha Real

South American Girl

Good Boy ~ Bad Boy

Opposites

Sunday In Queenz

Sinful

High Life / Fly Life

Money

My Bible

Ahead Of The Game

Powell Kline {Pt. 2}

My Baby Love

Daddy Dearest

A Tribute To Her

Bros Before Hos

No Hero

Tears

Embrace

The Solution {Pt. 1}

Unwrapped

Skydive

Blur

Libertivity

The Solution {Pt. 2}

7 Weapons

InsomniAddict

Get Familiar

Kali Dreamz

The Written Diss

Haikus About School

Them

Wedding Vows

Small World

(Reader discretion is strongly advised.)

Powell Kline {Pt. 1}

Eyes red as a stop sign, Mr. Kline cocked the nine

And choked on his bottle of moonshine…

Pine Sol colored H2O flowed from the faucet,

Standin' over the sink, he can't think, no mind

He's lost it.

Finds the light switch n' flicks it,

Sticks the barrel in his mouth, wife walks in & shouts,

"Powell don't!"

He wanna pull the trig but he won't;

So he pulls a 180 & focuses on his lady.

"Damn you ta Hell May!"

He sprays in her direction, hittin' the midsection;

Sound of the blast crashes throughout the sectioned apartment.

A harsh scent of hot lead spreads thru the air…

Powell stares at his wife in despair

She's scared, hopin' someone'll hear the fearful scene,

then in walks Irene

Screamin' at the sight of mommy on the bathroom tile…

Anotha shot fired, flies by the child's face

She turns away as she tries to escape and make it down the hallway.

"Honey wait!" Mr. Kline states, growin' more & more irate;

His boots skate over wifey's pool of red,

Her body grew colder the more she bled,

His daughter jets out the window, so

Ready for war, Kline jumps in his brother's Ford & floors it;

Poor Irene, unaware of where her fate will be put,

Still flees as fast as she can on foot.

Tears runnin' down her cheeks, she hears daddy's tires screech

To a freakish halt.

"Irene baby, this isn't your fault."

Full assault, Kline tightens his grip n' gets out the whip;

TriggA finga itchin' ta flip his lil girl world upside down.

Astounded by the sound of a click with no boom &

Eyes bulgin' like a cartoon's, Kline decides ta resume with the initial plan…

He scans and looks for his book of matches,

Snatches up a cigarette still drunk aza skunk n' goes for the Beretta his brotha keeps in the trunk…

Irene lil body gaspin' for oxy,

Approximately 30 secs go by and she lies down almost ready ta die;

Her father walks toward her with slow strides, he eyes his watch,

3:35 in the A.M.

He grins then attempts to loosen his buckle…

"Just lay there n' relax honey-suckle. We're gonna have some fun before you go."

FAR FROM OVER…

Faith

Day by day my fear grows of what's to come,

On a road to Darkness, someone help me find the sun;

The sun of a new day, of a new dawn,

Love that I thought would never die is crumbling & I don't know how to move on;

In a world where my hope has outrun me

But that hasn't stopped the kicks in my tummy,

What do I do? Where's my way?

Then I think to myself, could the answer be faith?

I Think it is.

(This poem is about an old friend of mine, who is very religious and happened to be pregnant at the time... pretty much in Desperate need of guidance.)

TrOuBlEd

Turn on my television... what's in ma vision?

Bad news, drunk broads n crooked politicians...

Who gunna break promises and shatter wishes...

The vicious cycle neva switches,

2 much heat & can't get out tha kitchen;

It's a neva endin drought... 2 many thirsty, hungry, empty mouths;

AIDS still buckwild n then u got the eye of the pedophile onya child...

Sleepless nights are lit by fiends lightin' pipes and

Just when you think you safe, you might not make it ta see the dawn's sunlight.

Cuz tha violence is rampant...

Bums beggin fa change on campuses,

This is C-H-A-O-S at its best and if you try to rest...

Shit... get arrested quick.

Jus ask Jena Six.

Ask America where's the peace and liberty.

Kinda goin' nowhere and just think of where these kids will be...

Little or no room fa chances cuz all they wanna do is f*ck,

act a fool and make up dances.

Havin fun but No advances... cuz we livin' in rubble,

Seems like the world is nothing but trouble;

We troubled.

(True, is it not?)

<u>NO LOVE</u>

No love ta niggaz pullin' triggaz just cuz Jeezy or Jigga said it,

No love ta Uncle Sam fa takin' down the twins n' sayin Osama did it…

No love ta closed minds rhymin' bout necks shinin' while their fatherless seed is at home cryin';

No love to a True BITCH who only afta ya riches and

gotta nerve ta leave you scratchin' n itchin'…

violatin' the pot that you piss in;   6☐

LISTEN!

No amour ta the boars who strike the ladies ta leave their souls broken and sore…

And LORD KNOWS,

Ain No love ta those who swear they above the rest cuza the religion they claim,

No love ta the shameless lames who used the word "love" just ta get their hands on some brain…

Brainless rapists n' racists are of a different breed and shall neva receive luv from me;

Neitha do the nuts who still bust nuts with bodies afta they dun already seen the lettaz H .I. V.

I'm sure u agree there's simply No L-O-V-E fa these diseases that we are

Forced to call

people.

Guess it turns out we're not all equal…cuz These MOTHAF*CKAZ…

GETS

NO

LOVE.

(Pardon My French.)

DEAR YOU KNOW WHO YOU ARE

WHERE DID ME N YOU GO WRONG?

THA DAYS WE HAD EACH OTHAZ HEARTS SINGIN SONGS ARE NOW LONG

GONE…

'EVERYTHING' AIN EVEN THE WORD FOR WHA U MEANT TA ME,

BUT NOW I SEE THAS DEAD; WE HISTORY.

ALL THAS LEFT TO DO IS REMINISCE OR LEAV IT ALONE…

AND IT SHOULD BE KNOWN THAT YOU COULDNT BE TOPPED BY ANY CHIC IN

MA PHONE;

IT WAS *YA* SLOT THAT HAD MA HEART.

AND DESPITE THE MILES APART, I WUZ WILLIN TO START SUTTN NEW WIT THA

ONLY LUV I GOT…

APPARENTLY SOMEBODY BEAT ME TO THE SPOT

A LOT SOONA THAN I THOUGHT.

I THOUGHT I WAS YA MOON & YOU WAS MY SUN…

THOUGHT WE WUD ALWAYS BE 1,

BUT NOW WE 2;

I NOW REALIZE LUV IZ PAIN AFTA LUVIN U.

BUT IM GOOD…ALWAYZ.

(peace)

THE COURTYARD

Pen in hand, ready ta set my canvas aflame…

Watchin dames walk by & act shy in fronta lames;

Hugs, kisses, dudes lookin for a Misses or jus kickin game fa sport…

Sportin cells n shell toes ta look fly in tha yard of the court;

Fort Knox when it comes to the ladies-

Some bars are real while the fool's gold stay shady;

Grady Memorial ambulance freelancing in the background,

But the sounds of friendship n laughter ring louder…

And even tho egos strut their shit- all prouda their Prada,

True beauty walks by and neitha sex can say nada.

Products of society eyein me while the leaders stay quiet and watch the scene…

Clean cut gentlemen & femmes in business attire wired thru Bluetooth,

Talkin' dollaz whetha their words are lies or truth…

seems like evry1 in a personal booth beggin ta leav;

but the sense of self is too stuck in its ways to be relieved.

I breathe in & breathe out as I see something I like

so iz time ta be out.

(Don't ever get Trapped in your own bubble.)

Daisy Dukes was still the shit back when I was wit this chic

Too young ta realize what I had so she disappeared like the era of black & white flix;

Now I see there's more chickenheads on the streets than in Colonel Sanders' coop...

Shoulda knew she was the truth, got me regrettin' that I eva threw her for a loop

Daisy G was the name of the dame that I wish I still claimed...

Every time I think of her it pours when it rains;

Ma brain don't rememba the face but I recall her grace,

The innocence that all of us sinners love to chase-

Seems like she was chasin' 30 while ma mind was still in the sandbox...

And on my heart, I would even let her sign the Hancock,

If she was still around...

But she ain't & I've found that she prolly neva will be.

Truth hurts and it's killin' me, but now I see Karma Alwayz

Intervenes...

And I truly believe I missed out on a prize & I don't care what any 'One' says,

it's never too late to apologize...

So I'm sorry Daisy baby;

Kisses & best wishes

(Always gotta know when you were wrong)

(Respect thy time.

THA REAL

"Go to college and get a good job."

The same old song that mobs the mind & robs it of its precious dream,

But it's seemingly what the caged bird always loves to sing;

Ever ready to clip ya wings and keep you grounded,

But F*CK…THAT. Get well-rounded.

Let the clowns remain dumbfounded & sound and act like they found 'it'.

'It'…the right way of life…

That path to success, happiness and a good husband or wife;

But when ya marriage is trife w/ less smiles than tears and it suddenly

appears that you starin' ya fears of failure in the eyes…

jus realize that it's prolly too late ta even relate ta ya once great aspirations.

You got the system tellin' you when to take a break when every day coulda been a vacation;

Black or white, you might not be pickin' cotton

but bet ya ass u on a plantation…

Coulda touched space but ya shuttle long gone n you stuck lookin' stupid at the station.

Stationed at ground level stayin' next ta gravity…

Shoulda listened ta tha voice unda ya chest cavity;

Cuz you NEVA postpone onya corazón.

THAS REAL.

South American Girl

Livin' in Brazil but she hail from Chilé.

Walkin' cold streets but the weatha's neva chillay.

Slayed bodies rot in every alley n' ditch and

Killin' n' dealin' the quickest ways ta get rich…

But not fa this South American chic whose only 13 but life already a bitch;

She stitchin' all the clothes for her lil brotha and sis...

Blistaz on her feet cuz the fam got few possessions and shoes ain on the list.

Missin' Poppa cuz Poppa's no longer aroun';

Pickpocket the wrong parta town & wha goes always comes back around & witta bigger sound…

Not ta mention Momma down and out cuz Malaria dun crawled up the water spout,

And when bad outnumbers good that's when you see what you really about.

So S.A.G goes out to church to hear the priest spit the gospel…

Then out to the streets to head right back to the brothel.

Hostile customers beat on her body & pride,

But they can't eva hurt her drive cuz the people at home gotta eat n' survive.

They gotta EAT & SURVIVE…

So like the worka bee in its hive,

she continues to strive…

Life aint all diamonds n pearls when you livin' a lifestyle like that of this

South American girl.

(Brazil is a crazy place.)

Good Boy ~ Bad Boy

Aight kid, u ready? You gotcha rubber inya pocket? ~

Shutcha ass up! Homie wanna hit it raw, why you trynna knock it?

I'm jus sayin though, don't you think safe is the way ta go nowadayz? ~

Man leave the boy alone, lil dude jus trynna get laid;

Wateva... anywayz... damn she smellin all good, least u know she clean ~

Nevamind her hygiene, get her out them tight ass jeans;

WOW, you peep the thong? Vic's Secret... the girl has class ~

Tru tru, now don b shy homie, u gotta make ya moves fast;

Damn... she all ova him, see I told you he dint havta give her no booze ~

Arigh u win that 1, now it's time 2 decide wha position 2 choose;

Wait, wait, wait, don put it in yet, u ain got no protection ~

I dun toldja ass once before! Jus let tha boy enjoy his erection;

Okay, WATCH... the kid gunna catch somethin or get her pregnant. You have any sense? Cuz i cant tell ~

Negro please, that chic ain got no STDz & is the word abortion ringin' any bells?

Look at u, thinkin' wit ya dingaling insteada ya damn brain! ~

Don listen 2 him homie, he been a virgin all his life & he ain eva gunna change;

Wha the hell u doin? You gotta pull out! Sex is ova, stop bein a fiend ~

Mannn, shut ya dumb ass up...

kid jus havin a wet dream.

("Neva know what you gonna do when ya in the pinch." -P.E.)

12

OPPOSITES

One is in it fa lust

One lustin fa love;

One is willin ta trust

One freakin the clubs;

Yet that one want security

And this one wanna live free;

One livin fairy tales, the otha livin Tragedy…

One preach Rebelution but tha otha say "Yes ya Majesty."

Such a travesty that the person in the mirror

Has a habit of bein ya opposite…

But don't eva make them ya opposition.

play YA position

(Never follow boys and girls, never follow)

13

<u>Sunday</u>
<u>In</u>
<u>Queenz</u>

Half asleep, cold chills creepin up my spine

So I grip the sheets n pull em ova the

Nappy head I had at the time;

Cracks of sunshine beamin thru the dusty shades,

Eyes still in a sleepy haze but my nose kno breakfast is bein made…

My daze interrupted cuz the aroma itself is fillin

Climb out the bed to find pigeons cooin on tha window sill

Straight chillin…

Villains runnin' amuck

So on occasion, sirens ring w/ the rumble of the garbage truck;

Chickens cluckin 5 stories below,

but lil girlz ain on tha mind, im more concerned wit whas on the stove.

So over to a clean sink brushin the pearly whites

Cuz Momz & Ajax got tha baño shinin' bright.

Right to the table afta wishin tha folks a good mornin'

Said the grace right away cuz I wasn't trynna hear no scornin;

& its mornings like these that make me wanna be born again cuz

Damn…

Im missin QuEeNz.

(I'll always luv tha Q)

14

<u>SINFUL</u>

All you think about is sex.

You eat way too damn much.

All you want is money.

You don't do shit.

You're always desiring what you can't have.

You put yourself on a damn pedestal.

And there's not a day that goes by that your heart isn't filled with hate!

But wait...hold up...

Was that a twenty you just put in the collection plate?

Well shiyyit...for you, maybe we do have a place;

Take a seat in a pew, the sermon begins in a few.   15

(HaHa)

HIGH LIFE/FLY LIFE

Life…

Don't want the good, jus the high & the fly

We spendin like we made it and we dont kno why;

Why we livin in a condo and don't kno where tha rent at?

Why dough keep runnin low and we don't rememba where it's spent at?

Cuz we trynna liv the high life

That fly life

Wanna shine like the Chi-Lites

Or make a quick 100 mill like Shaq wife

Hungry nights might have the stomach in knots

But thas all good once we takin shots on a 3 story yacht

The top is the only spot we wanna rock wit

Thas why we reachin even fartha & pushin even harda cuz

We wanna push Benzos,

F*ck ridin MARTA

We smarta than that

Much too large to be in that same ol' boat

And on that note, I'd like ta thank the Almighty for our daily bread

But everyone knows ain't nothin like havin sum butter around ta spread…

Therefore, the higher flyer life is where we headin.

(Just Watch)

MONEY

Money…

The issue of the ages;

Justa piece of paper but still valued more than the precious

Pages of a book,

Cuz the look and feel of that green inya hands is grand

But in such high demand that you can't stand it when ya funds

Jus ain't expandin' & you landin in a hole.

Bodies of sold souls holdin ya cash

As you watchin ya stash dwindle.

That feelin of security with which you can't re-kindle…

Kinda crazy that it's only a piece of paper but we make her

RULE THE WORLD

She's everyone's favorite girl,

And we just swirl around her

Lookin done and dumb…

But since it's on this Earth, might as well get up

Get out n GET SOME.

(FIND YA GRIND.)

MY BIBLE

SYZ!QUE 3:16

MAKE IT HAPPEN…

No matta how long it takes

Every negative is a positive

Just learn from *every* mistake.

The World IS YOURS so TAKE it

Instead of only taking what you can get…

And neva eva forget to Always stay humble and always stay tru

Even though ya fate &destiny is all in YOU;

So Make It Happen!

No one stops you.

Nothin' breaks you.

You a Classic

You the Truth

And this is all true cuz

I AM YA BIBLE.

(I read it every day.)

7 WEAPONS

TwO hands ta tote tools of wisdom & prosperity

OnE tongue ta speak only tha real & words of sincerity;

5 senses & a sense of clarity is provided by the

OnE precious mind we carry without a price;

And we walk on TwO legs fa safe travel to our personal paradise...

The one heaven that our OnE heart is hell-bent on getting to.

You'll get there.

Trust...

But we must be reminded

Not to be blind to the fact that

these are in Fact...

WeApOns.

(Use them for the good or use them for the ugly. YOU choose.)

INSOMN!ADDICT

While the rest of the world lies in its deepest sleep,

I creep into my bed, eyes weary , appearing reaped.

They weep after screaming at my lids to stay shut...

But of course, no luck.

Once that clock struck midnight noon I was

Doomed to be up

And STAY up

Til the sun up makes me shut tha blinds so

I'm not blinded by the sharp glisten.

On a mission cuz missin out on good Zzz's

Isn't justa disorder,

Iza disease.

Easily leavin' me restless, depressed n'

STRESSED

I try to stretch it out & my body expresses

Its profound frustration w/ me...

Then the prickly heat behind the spheres of my eyes

Defeats my desire to fight it anymore.

Energy falls n hits the floor

Til I wake up again, bored out of my mind cuz I

Can't find a way to turn off the anxiety

That grinds my nerves and drives me up a wall.

Duz insomnia say it all?

Is that the only reason I'm so deprived?

Or is it because I'm just So Addicted to being

ALiVE…

(Don't really sleep enough to have many dreams, so I have no choice but to live most of mine)

GET FAMILIAR

Familia faces

always gracin you w/ their presence

effervescently…

whetha the bond be sweet or sour,

believe it or not yall were meant ta be,

for the company you keep is

the company you bring…

clingin to the heart

hangin ta the soul

the real ones stick around &

the fakes' shoulders stay cold.

It's a Cold world we live in Ladies & Gents…

Every day is a familia battle so dig ya trench.

And neva repent cuz what is meant to be will B,

And I don't mean to repeat but this is all

TRUTH ma words speak;

And though at times,

I may find a shrinking flame on the future's candle

I still resort to grabbin' a pen over a Gun handle…

Now handle that

And GET FAMILIAR.

(Get used to this)

KaLi Dreamz

Cali Dreamin again…

Itz becomin a personal trend;

The enda ma lens got the Pacific in sight

So I jus might have ta satisfy myself witta flight,

And im na speakin roundtrips

Cuz im neva 1 wit goin in circles,

Justa worthless waste of time and hoppin' hurdles

And it's MuRda she Wrote once im strokin' ma fingaz

thru tha Shores of Santa Món…

in ma zone, gettin blown away by waves

of green, white and grey vegetation

straight from the MeJiCaNo NaTion…

skatin' on cloud 105 drivin' pretty ladies wild

while I scheme n' plan on how ta take ova LaLa Land…

and I can't stop

won't stop

Cali Dreamin'… Not a chance

(Going going ~ Back back)

Kiss ma ass!

I neva liked you from the get-go

I see you & ya girl lookin like yall do all ya shoppin at PETCO;

But anyway…

YO

Let go of the hope that you gonna find the one

Cuz we wouldn't want the otha kids to poke and make fun at ya

funny ass lookin' daughters n sons;

And how about you keep a loaded gun in case you eva

Wanna be done wit it & delete yaself;

Complete the self-development list and release yaself…

That selfish lil Biznitch you always been.

It should be a mortal sin to walk around inya shoes and

Lose any dignity you had since the womb…

A stink ass Dirty womb at that

Cuz ya birth ain't have much of an audience but ya Momz had the CLAP!

Matta fact, scratch that…

clap ya hands, make me snap out of it,

I kno God don't like ugly…

But then again, ya ugly ass is make believe

Jus like ya homegirl weave,

you ain even real…jus real stupid n stubby

u a joke

Go play with the Teletubbies.

Now pop some bubbly;

Cuz This concludes the summary of a written diss.

CLaSS Dismissed…

LATA.

(Haters aren't such bad people when they don't exist)

Haikus ABOUT School

Sex, Smoke and knowledge,

Thousands with changing goals,

Only in college...

Playground for pupils...

Ramen noodles and people

Who cease to learn shit

Chasing the degree

Taste of freedom tastes so good

Just want to be free

(I wanna go to Tokyo)

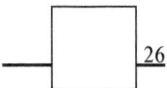

THEM

They did this…they did that.

How long can you blame *them* for where *you* at?

Get back ta doin you more,

Even if you Have been the victim once or twice before.

Stop storin' hate or you'll jus end up in all the wrong places

Soon findin' that the puzzle u call life is creatin' less pieces than spaces…

Age gracefully

And move up in the right direction

Only then will we bridge all the gaps & make the right connections;

Count ALL ya blessinz n stop stressin ova the he say-she say,

Thas fa kids at play with nothin betta ta do,

So quit worryin about Them

Start thinkin bout U…

(Mind Ya F*ckn Business, fareal.)

Wedding Vows

Dangerous…

My pride's been stabbed

There's a bad habit I can't seem ta drop

And I don't kno howda stop it;

Stop this fixation when there is no rehabilitation.

Take a break they say , but I can't break the cycle of thinkina

YOU

I'm passed the brink of crazy, I been flew the coop;

You the music of my life & iza neva endin loop.

Round and roun' the world turns as my heart yearns

To burn every second of ma life w/ ma otha half,

Half the time with you is laughter n tha otha…

Pure bliss

Your kiss is all I need ta get ta that satisfactory state

That taste of heaven that elevates me to a

State of mind unparallel ta any otha kind.

No need in even trynna deny it…

I guess what I'm trynna say is…

28

I love you baby girl…

I love you.

MmmWa

(No Time Soon)

Small World

Ay, u eva thnk about how some parents brag about their kidz w/ such vane,
One perfect example, tha otha day I was headed 2 Queenz NY,

ridin tha R train;
A groupa ladies wuz discussin how proud they were of their baby girls,
3 white women & 1 black, 2 had their hair str8,
1 had tha hair tied back & tha black lady jus got her hurr curled;
"My baby jus graduated from high school, now tha possibilities are endless of what she can be.
She talks of goin' ta NYU & pickin' up herself a nice business degree."
"That's nice. Well Kim plannin' on goin' ta cosmetology school," said tha black chic w/ tha curly hair.
"She gonna grow up to own her own shop, that damn girl can BRAID, lemme tell you, I swear."
Tha woman smiled, tha otha ladies gave their fake smiles too;
I was jus waitin' 4 them to take out photos so ica see who looked betta than who;
I started to nod off until 1 of tha ladies w/ str8 hair opened her mouth n' announced,
"Well Veronica is a gold medal gymnast at her school, she gonna go to this fancy academy down south."
I noticed that tha last ladyz face started 2 look uneasy,
Tha sweat started to roll & her face started lookin' greasy;
She said quietly,
"Well I don have anything to brag about like tha resta you guys,
Ya see, insteada bein' into guys' arms & abs,

Abby's more into girl's curves & thighz;

Yeah, my little girl is a Lez, I must confess.

But I must say, as far as her 'girlfriend' goes,

my daughter is blessed;

Her girl just graduated & she's already kinda jaded.

She buys her clothes & perfume…does my daughter's hair whenever she wants it braided;

I neva really thought anotha female could make my baby feel this fantastic,

Hell, tha damn grl even teaches Abby gymnastics."

I tried so hard to keep a str8 face, but in ma mind I wuz havinna bALL,

That chic's daughter prolly had tha otha 3 as we speak,

Doin tha durrty while their mommas were righ here lookin' all appalled;

So overall, they *all* gay, guess you can't knock,

They *all* munchin' that magic carpet, thinkin' inside tha box;

Small ass world afta All…

(Not a true story but I'm sure it is somewhurr.)

HOME ALONE

Last day of tha summa, dude got tha crib all 2 himself,

Parents gonna b gone 4 awhile, homie don kno wha 2 do w/ his self;

Where tha phone at? He got sum numbaz ta call,

He ain trynna please himself all alone,

hell na, not at all;

One tired & wanna go straight ta sleep,

anotha one iz cookin & gettin ready 2 eat,

One iz bein stupid & ain answerin' her phone,

Damn...

1 last numba & Finally...

chic is hot n' bothered, ready 2 bone;

She on her way over so he gotta do a lil cleanin',

Excited, anticipatin' tha pleasure, homeboy iz feenin;

Momma calls & says they gonna b home a lil late,

bad traffic n bad weatha on tha interstate;

But in ain no biggie Ma.Ya boy got his self a cute ass date;

Tha door bell rings, ahhh shyt, iz boutta b on n PoPp!N,

Mos definitely,

Good Lord, can't wait fa dat ol' fashioned TLC;

Afta a lil convo, they easin' up tha stairs,

Uh-oh...nobody gotta rubba...shyt...

f*ck it, WHO CARES;

They end up in tha bathroom of all places,

Tha shower's turned on & steam starts ta cover their faces;

Panties & drawz hit tha floor, her legs lockd aroun' his waist,

Hoppin' in tha showa butt ass naked & ain no time ta waste;

Hot water hittin their bodies, things gettin' drippin' n soakin' wet,

Wit all the kissin, suckin, n' lickin, this as good as it could possibly get;

Tha fun is ova afta awhile, dude happy he lasted that long,

They dry up & go 2 sleep, he in his boxaz & she inna thong;

Wake up in tha bright mornin sun ta tha phone ringin',

Bad newz homie, ya folks wuz inna wreck las nigh, tha fat lady iz singin;

NO, this can't b tha reason they neva came home las nigh,

Mad at tha world, mad at himself, he tight & ready 2 fight;

Afta nights of mourning, tha guilt builds up & tha facts are revealed,

While he was in tha showa gettin ass, his momz wuz flyin thru a windshield;

Not only does he grow up without parents in a world of distortion,

But he gon havta raise a kid since him and his lil chic cant afford an abortion;

Now he wishes he was neva home alone,

Now lil dude iz all on his own,

all on his own...

(Take Nothing and No One for granted)

AHEAD OF THE GAME

WHY…do i find myself writin books n bumpin beats while ma brothaz runnin tha streets,

slayin' their otha brothaz who aint got shit ta eat?

Where tha hopes? Where all tha goals? Where tha f*ck alla dreams at?

And insteada givin tha next dude a hand, we wanna look down on & laugh at 'em;

Niggaz thinkin' bout gettin ahead but neva wanna expand they damn knowledge,

Some aint got tha dough ta do so but some who do won't even pick up a Book,

much less apply ta college.

With that shit bein said, f*ck it, Ima say it…

I'm ahead.

I was tha first ta tap that chic Eve, nevamind wha Adam said;

And she was worth every minute, i gotta admit.

Shez stilla liar though,

I baked a personal pie with tha apple she claim she bit;

And back in the day, I stayed bein' the talk of the town,

Ma boy Father Time stayed beggin' me ta slow down,

but I just moved on, intentions unannounced.

I even gave them cave dudes a light ta spark tha first fire,

Had tha 1st queens feedin' me grapes and tha 1st kings callin' Me sire;

Not ta mention, I put up tha signs sayin'

"Pharoahs and Gods for hire"

AND for tha last supper I was the supplier of every piece of bread and every glass of wine,

Jeaa you're pretty much inclined ta say that

I'm kinda heada tha times...

(Just felt like being cocky)

Powell Kline {Pt. 2}

"Daddy no…" Irene sobbed slowly

She continued ta gasp as she grasped Poppa's pant leg.

"Stop it Irene; you know better than ta beg."

He hit her once & clinched her legs, put the Retta on the curb.

But before he could insert his piece of perversion into his virgin little girl,

The boys in blue curled aroun' the corna…

Kline picked up the heat & hurled 4 shots.

Aimed ta kill, the slugs were unstopped by the windshield

And popped 1 cop, leavin' his top lopsided;

His partna decided ta get out…

Ouchin' over the smokin' holes in his shoulder & chest…

"Should have wore a vest," Kline thought to himself.

He felt his self gettin' a little sober so he headed back over

Ta the back seat of the Ford…

Looked down at his watch, 3:44,

Tore into his bottle of Shine and took his time getting' back ta

Irene who was traumatized by this neva endin' bad dream.

Kline depleted the bottle n' dropped it right before it cracked on the concrete.

Still intent on skeetin', he dropped to his knees & eased his mind ta get aroused…

Powell's baby girl found stayin' conscious kinda hard but she still spotted a shard of glass not

too far from her position;

Before he knew it, Mr. Kline was missin' a piece of his pisser,

Wishin he neva listened ta the sinister voices in his head.

Screamin his head off, he had the whole hood listenin' to him writhe in pain…

In about 4 seconds, 5 frames, it started ta rain on the blood-stained scenario;

Irene stands on her own two, her feet now very cold…

But she doesn't let it hold her back from escapin' this wicked place--

Sight of his daughter starts ta fade and Powell's lungs slowly fail to inflate.

She awakes…

Awakes from the nightmare that's haunted her in her night terrors & fears afta many years in the

Psyche ward;

She now realizes that

Life & Death

are double-edged swords.

THE END

The following poems are contributions from my sistaz & brothaz of a different mother and of course, color. These individuals, just like you, possess POTENTIAL beyond even their own recognition. Here is their artwork of words. Read carefully and keep an open mind at all times. This is family. Enjoy.

My Baby Love

It was late September when I found out you were there,

And I must admit I was VERY scared…

You came to me with such a surprise

Almost every day you brought tears to my eyes.

Not because I hated you or didn't want you there,

But because I Loved You, wished above the stars for you & wanted you

Everywhere…

My baby love, I hope that you can forgive me some day

And I Never wanted you to go away.

My heart was filled with love for you;

I loved you even before you were there…

And not a day goes by that I don't think about you

So please don't Ever think that I didn't care.

I think and imagine about how you must look…

Your hair, your eyes, your smell, your smile;

Forever thinking about the times we could have shared…

Your first words, your first steps…even your high chair

It was All out of love.

And I know you're a little angel in the heavens up above,

Walking hand in hand with our Creator cuz remember…

you were made from love.

For you my sweet, until we meet…

My Baby Love

Cookie   1/19/97

Daddy Dearest

Daddy Dearest what have you done to me??

I'm not the little girl I used to be;

The one that once ran into your arms…

The one you once thrilled with all your charm.

Daddy Dearest what have you done to me?

You're not the man you seemed to be.

You left me with a heart So sad,

And in my mind were thoughts So mad.

I turned to you for love, support and guidance

But all you left me was a remembrance of what Could have been.

Daddy Dearest, What Have You Done To Me???

You're not the man you Should have been;

And as for me, I'll never be the same again.

And while you're in your Shitty ass home, all alone

With your drugs to keep you company…

Do you ever think about ME?

Do you remember when you made your little girl cry?

Do you remember when you said goodbye?

Can you remember the girl you left behind?

Do You Hear Me Daddy?

Cookie 4/18/96

40

A Tribute To Her

I saw the morning dew in the sunrise

Reminiscent of your dark brown eyes

For they glisten oh so gently

Like stars in the midnight skies

Your skin is the hue of honey and milk,

A mixture I long to taste…

Your touch is as delicate as silk

But you persist to make me wait

Where did you come from? Why are you here? What do you want from me?

My friendship? My time? My money? My love?

…or is it ecstasy?

I'll give it all to you, no question…you only have to ask

I just hope in this race for your love, I don't finish last

You are so unique in your ways

Like this poem, you take on different shapes

No certain pattern, no certain rhyme,

But in writing this I took my time

For these words are a tribute to you

My sunrise, my star, my morning dew.

R. English

<u>Bros Before Hos</u>

We say bros before hos, but that's not really so…
Cuz when a dude gets to know one, the bro is the first to go
All his time is wrapped in his new found mate
Swearing up and down that he and she are fate;
He closes off his senses to the world of common sense,
Steady tellin' him she ain't no good but that boy ain't hearin' SHIT-

Judgment and observation fly away, and she shoots them out the sky…
Using words and her body, she pulls wool over his eyes;
Now he's trapped in HeR world & she *swallows* the key to the lock…
He could break free of his prison, but he's only thinking with the cock.
His friends have given up on him. "Let him find out for himself.
When he sees her skeezin', he'll put the ho on his shelf."

So for months and months, he's led by lust n' controlled by strings,
He even hits up the jeweler for an engagement ring.
Til all of a sudden his world is crushed and the truth hits him hard…
Catches his so called love in the food court tonguing the security guard

He says nothing…
he just goes home to think of who was once his future wife;
Sits on the edge of the bed w/ a blade & decides to try and take his life.
So sad that he lost himself over his love & there's no 2nd chance…
Respect the code. Bros before hos. Hear your mind before your pants.

R. English

42

<u>No Hero</u>

I don't have wings, i haven't stuttered or hesitated,

that joint i smoked was the last time i levitated.

So why is everything i do ridiculed and denigrated?

no matter how much i pour in, the public's Never satiated.

I rep chi-town from my head to my feet

While you walked the straight line i ran mazes in the streets.

7 figures later… my life's doing a figure 8

i can't even roll with models with this role model cape.

Jayson D.

40tree

Tears
By Aja Morris

Falling…running down
my cheek.
Crying, hurting, pain
from someone I love.
It's crazy how much it hurts, how
Could you fill me with so much pain?
You love me, so you say,
But your kind of love can sting.
Tears, they fall, they stain
My face and wet my eyes.
They look invisible from afar, but
Burn on the inside.
My heart, it hurts…it probably wouldn't be so bad
If it wasn't you that made these tears fall.
If I didn't love you so much, i
Probably wouldn't care at all.
The tears…they stop, they
Begin again.
So much damage…it's killing me,
When will it end?
My heart…it's broken…but not for long.
You hurt me so much that I did it.
I ended it.
My life…it's through,
I feel no more pain.
The tears they don't fall, they don't burn,
They don't stain.
Me…the stinging…Gone.

I'm finally free.
No more crying…
No more tears running down my cheek.
No more tears!

Embrace
By Aja Morris

Feeling you, feeling me

Wrapped in this moment

We both should be.

Happiness is showing all over my face.

Feeling your arms, caught in your warm embrace.

Your skin so brown, I'm loving your

Soft touch…

Your eyes so deep, I love you so much.

You're taking me to a level I've never seen.

Me wrapped up in you, and you

Continuously loving me.

My first time, I never thought

It would be you.

You fulfilled my every need, my

Dreams came true.

You read my mind and followed my

Expressions.

You made sure you were gentle

And threw away all aggression.

Looking into your eyes, seeing the ecstasy

In your face.

Still loving you, feeling an even

Warmer embrace.

Lying in your arms, overtaken

By your charm,

Thinking to myself that this love is true.

Saying to myself

"He must really love you."

We've been together for a while.

And even the slightest glance from you

Makes me smile.

I'm listening to the beating of your heart.

It's funny how we knew we were

In love from the start.

While you're asleep I kiss your gentle face.

Then I fall back into your warmest

Embrace.

The Solution {Part I}

I have a solution in mind

To this hate and turmoil which afflicts mankind

And it's not immediate to cause peace

But over time it will ease the pain

Like a cool rain running down the cheek

Of some beggar you might meet

And judge because we all do

But we're not right to

Because even though he may not lead life like you would

Do you think you could

Swallow your pride and beg for a dime

To feed your addiction

That heals your affliction and hurt

Of being all alone with no one to turn to

I know I couldn't

I'd like to think I wouldn't

But I'd prob'ly just give up

And shoot up but prob'ly take it one step further

Overdose and murder myself

To escape myself

But more importantly this world that turns without you

You think it cares about you, but it doesn't

If you think it was good to you, it wasn't

You just got lucky

Just be ready, because luck runs out.

Everyone's trying to change

To become the same

But they don't realize how insane that is

We need to celebrate our differences

Only then can we exist together

Learn and grow from each other

Making the world better.

Kyle M.

Unwrapped

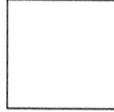

I can't take it anymore,

I want a divorce.

I'm tired of being forced to

Help you all the time.

I've got *my* own self to worry about

Yet, I can't have a day without you dragging me down

And burning my soul to the ground with your issues

Grab a Tissue

I'm tired of helping you

I want out

I'm sick of your mouth

And getting nothing but lip in return

You'd better learn how to cope on your own

'Cause I'm gone.

Kyle M.

..Skydive..

"Any first time is always tough,"
He told her with a grin.
But I'll be here if things get rough
Sit back, enjoy the wind

He told her not to worry much
It doesn't hurt to land
He's only here to be a crutch
Enjoy as best you can

Just close your eyes and take a breath
And get close to the line
Then make your dive into the depths
And freefall through the sky

For when you land, you'll always know
Just how great it is
But if you can, approach it slow
Learn from past captives

Know if you use it for a rush
It's purpose you've confound
And from experience lost trust
Feet staying on the ground.

Kyle M.

Blur

We need to grey the lines of black and white

To make it just wrong and right

Because it's not what I'm doing tonight

It's color that helps me along

It's clear to see there's something wrong

With society today

Wonder why people keep running away

From their problems

Instead of trying to solve them

Because they're right when they say

That the system doesn't help them the way it helps me

But at the same time their problems lie inside

Because nothing's being changed within

When life's a perpetual sin

You've got to help yourself first

And that can cause the worst pain

Leave some people out in the worst rain

When life's the only thing to gain

And death's the only thing to fear

And everyday it's getting nearer

Things become clearer

And you realize what's important

That life is short and

To make things different

You've got to drop some of this hate

Use some of that money you make

And rain it on someone in need

Help each other and try to lead

People in the right direction

So the next generation

Has some more respect and intelligence

To live with a little less "race"

And die with a little more grace

And leave the world a better place…

Kyle M.

<u>Libertivity</u>

The truth hurts the worst when it's close to home

It can make you feel so lonely

It completely disregards your plans

And acts like it's the only thing that matters

Because it's so flattered

That it can batter *you* up and bruise *me*

Sayin', "You won't ever be able to lose me,

And even though you didn't choose me,

I'm here."

And it's not going anywhere

But we're still looking everywhere to find it

Keeping in mind that

It can shine some light

When it's too dark to see

That the truth can set you free.

Kyle M.

54

The Solution {Pt. II}

I have a solution in mind
To this hate and turmoil which afflicts mankind
Maybe not directly but we all feel it somehow
And we want to heal it but we don't know how
The world's such a small place today
So many different things play a part
So many different faces that belong to so many different races
But we need to embrace them
Not just cast them aside with a snide look
Because we're all hooked on ourselves
Just look past yourself for once
Open your eyes to the ones around us
You were once there
We all came from somewhere across the world
In today's global economy
We're stuck in immobile monotony
Slowly getting left behind
We've come so far together
United we stand, divided we fall together
It's a shame it takes tragedy to realize we're all together
And without each other
We have nothing.
Everyone's trying to change
To become the same
They don't realize how insane that is
We need to celebrate our differences
Only then can we exist together
Learn and grow from each other

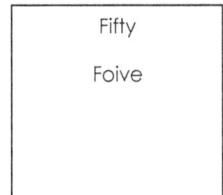

Fifty
Foive

MAKING THE WORLD BETTER.

Contributors

Keisha "Cookie" Mahboob
Aja Lewis
Rashad English
Jayson Dowell
Kyle McFarland
&
Kevin J. Lamont

In loving memory of
Trae W. Cagle
Live on in nothing but eternal peace

This is only the beginning…